I0539340

St. Andrews Review

The 50th Anniversary Issue

Edited by

Ted Wojtasik

Copyright © St. Andrews University Press 2018

All Rights Reserved

No part of this work may be reproduced or transmitted in any form or by any means, electronic or mechanical, including photocopying and recording, or by any information storage or retrieval system without the proper written permission of the copyright owner unless such copying is expressly permitted by federal copyright law.

Front cover art: Dobree Adams
Design and typesetting: Ted Wojtasik
Proofreader: Sanita Edwards

ISBN-13: 978-0999787359
ISBN-10: 0999787357

UNIVERSITY
PRESS

St. Andrews University Press

St. Andrews University
(A Branch of Webber International University)
1700 Dogwood Mile
Laurinburg, NC 28352
press@sa.edu
(910) 277-5310

Editorial Board

Paul Baldasare
Joseph Bathanti
Richard Blanco
Betsy Dendy
Robert Hopkins
Edna Ann Loftus
Madge McKeithen
Ted Wojtasik

Ted Wojtasik, Editor

Ronald H. Bayes, Founding Editor
1969

Dedicated to

the Founding Editor Ronald H. Bayes,
whose vision we have been following ever since

Table of Contents

Editor's Note

It has been my great pleasure to edit the 50th anniversary issue of *St. Andrews Review* with such grand and outstanding poems, essays, and fiction. The theme of the issue was based upon the artistic vision of Black Mountain College with those directly involved— Jonathan Williams, Basil King, and Martha King—and those who have been influenced by its spirit of innovation, excellence, and passion.

—Ted Wojtasik

Jonathan Williams

Samaras–Not Saharas

Dobree Adams stays down on the farm, and then looks down: snow in a tire rut and whiz/bang, there's an upsidedown forest... Meanwhile, over there masses of pear blossoms busy themselves constructing a geometric critter with a long face and a long neck... and, as for the samaras, they are turning themselves into two Japanese demons about to attack each other... In these modest pools of water we walk amidst, it is all happening.

Maybe Dobree can tell us why Jean-Phillipe Collard, the brilliant French pianist, has the same name as that strong Southern vegetable: collards, a variety of kale, *Brassica oleracea acephala*? Monsieur Collard eateth nary no collards, but every time I see the word *collards* I am thrown into another sonic universe. I welcome these jolts, but often have to scratch my head. Language is banging heads all the time. But, let's let Jean-Phillipe tickle Monsieur Poulenc's ivories.

Those who have read Philip Pullman's magnificent trilogy, *His Dark Materials*, will respond to the idea of parallel worlds: "Will knew without the slightest doubt that that patch of grass on the other side was in a different world. He couldn't possibly have said why. He knew it at once, as strongly as he knew that fire burned and kindness was good. He was looking at something profoundly alien."

Watch PBS these days and see programs with physicists in their labs working on "string theory" and the idea of "branes" that are parallel to us in the universe. Dobree Adams's photography takes what's there under our feet and makes it all be seen anew, from other sides.

As e.e. cummings concluded in one of his very best poems "pity this busy monster, manunkind":

We doctors know

a hopeless case if—listen: there's a hell
of a good universe next door; let's go

Dobree Adams

Mrs. Sadie Grindstaff, Weaver and Factotum, Explains the Work-Principle to the Modern World

I figured
anything anybody
could do a lot of I
could do a little
of

mebby

—BLUES & ROOTS / RUE & BLUETS

In a past life, in the world of computers, my secretary was coaxed and commissioned to needlepoint Ms. Grindstaff for my studio. There she is now, hovering above my walnut loom.

Trips to Highlands are full of memories of waterfalls and Jargon Society picnics, Tom's delightful cooking and of the gracious Georgette, whom I met at Corn Close in 1974, on our honeymoon trip. A. Doyle Moore was there, too, knitting or tatting away.

On that honeymoon trip we visited Peter Rabbit's garden and Beatrix Potter's home with Georgette and JW who also introduced me to wool of the Herdwick sheep and saw that we had a proper crook, made of haw with a ram's horn handle, from Mr. Bob Johnson, one of the last local stickmakers thereabouts. My notes from that trip are full of quotes from Anni Albers' *On Designing* and Edward Weston's *Fifty Years*. Early influences.

Over these 30 years, JW has introduced me to galax and Bartram's *Franklinia* at Skywinding, and dovedale moss and wild thyme on a Fell End Clouds walk. Likewise, to trods (sheep paths) and triddlings (what you find there). My endless curiosity about plants, their shapes, textures, colors has been whetted by JW's encyclopedic knowledge of what's out there, from samaras to topiary gardens, cairns and stone circles.

By 1994 I was seriously attached to my camera and shooting 35mm slides, documenting what would be the influences behind my woven work. At Corn Close once again I was taking solitary walks along the road or scampering in the bracken above the house. Always to come back with questions about the plants I had met along the way.

Jonathan and I have shared a common culture of the South, both having been brought up on the likes of collards and turnip greens, grits, biscuits, cornbread, and sippin' whiskey. In untold ways inspiration and nurturing from Jonathan have always been there for me, from the first slide shows of his work and the first walk in the Smokies.

Onward, JW! Here's to 75 and more to come!

Basil King

My First Black Mountain

It was the day the day
Day Lilies bloom
But it wasn't
It was the day
My mother and I
Came to Black Mountain
It was September 1951
I was sixteen
And my mother came with me

Pause

The table was set on the lawn opposite the dining hall
with China cups and saucers a tablecloth and a silver
teapot. Some of Black Mountain's European faculty
spoke with my mother and I can't remember being
spoken to. It wasn't until my mother got up and said "You
are going to like it here" and asked was it possible for her
to get a ride back to Asheville that the faculty asked me
about myself. Later I was introduced to Joe Fiore. I had
been asked to bring a sample of my work. I showed Joe a
painting of a boy stretched out on a beach with a large
banana next to him. Joe said, "I guess we all have our
surreal period."

Pause

I was seven. My mother was to have an operation. My
father had to work and there was no one in the family

who could take care of me. The Montague sisters were wealthy twins on the board of the Maude Nathan Home, a small Jewish boarding school modeled after Summerhill School in the beautiful country side of Essex. It was expensive. My father was very well thought of in the Jewish community in London and the sisters paid my tuition. And we all called it the Home.

Pause

The boys and girls ranged from 6 to 13 years old. There were two young orphans. I can't remember any one coming to see them. Whereas the rest of us had periodic visits from mothers, fathers, aunts and uncles. A number of the children came from very wealthy homes. Stanley's father owned a number of Barber Shops.

Pause

Jackie was my age and her mother and father drove down at least once a month in a red Buick with white sidewalls and a chauffeur. It was 1943 in the middle of the war and they would bring chickens and food bought on the Black Market. The Matron would have the cook make chicken soup from one of the chickens. The Matron, the head nurse, and the Matron's daughter ate the chicken. We never saw it again. We heard that all the other food had been sold to the locals. The war had taken the original staff and teachers into the army. As for the faculty I think there were two teachers who were English, the remaining faculty were highly educated refugees from Europe.

Pause

The Montague sisters came to the Home from London in their chauffeur-driven limousine every other month. They would ask for the "Cohen boy." The sisters were tall and were always dressed alike in Edwardian clothing. They always carried handbags and wore little hats. They would ask me what classes I was taking, what was I reading and they wanted to see my drawings. We never sat down and they would look at the drawings and smile. I stood in front of them and when I looked up there were always food stains on their blouses.

Pause

There was playtime and we could grow anything we wanted on our own plot of land. I grew Sunflowers. There was a gardener straight out of an English novel. He lived on the grounds in a small shack, constantly smoked a pipe, and answered questions with different grunts.

Pause

At the Home we were together and we were alone, without our parents we depended on ourselves, and the guidance of strangers. Being at the Home was an initiation that would remain with me for the rest of my life. The classes were small there were five to six of us in a class sometimes there would be only three. Years after my mother's operation and her convalescence she said she was sorry that she hadn't saved my letters. She said that they were so detailed that she read them out loud to the other ladies.

Pause

Runners pace
Race Drivers pace
Boxers pace
Jockeys pace
Fox's pace

Not everyone wants to go at their own pace it has nothing to do with intelligence. But what it does have to with is giving, of asking, of finding things, things that might cause conflict and might not be automatically successful. No one taught art at the Home but there was a European woman who taught math who was knowledgeable about art she would talk to me about my drawings.

Pause

I had tutorials in history with a young German who later became a Rabbi. He read Holbein's letters to me in German. I've forgotten my Yiddish but at age seven I was able to follow most of what he was reading and what I didn't understand he translated. If he read it to me in a letter or showed it to me in photographs when Martha and I were in Basel Switzerland I walked up an alley that was on a hill and when I got to the top I was bewildered. I knew I'd been here before. But when? There was the University, St. George and the Dragon, the Cathedral, and the view of the Rhine. And it took two return trips to remember what I was seeing had been given to me in one of the tutorials.

Pause

The first thing I learned
At Black Mountain College
Was "The sky is blue"
Delivered to me by Fielding Dawson
After he had read
And crossed out the excess
I had included in a short piece
Of prose written for class
Painting, poetry, pottery
History and prose
Before the dance

Lift up your dress
Take down your pants
Geography
Freedom and intensity
I said to myself
Children know the seasons
I've been here before

Pause

What I learned at the Home was a blessing and a curse. I learned to work at my own pace and devour what I wanted. What I wanted was History and Art. And I thought I knew everything. It was years after leaving Black Mountain and having internalized everything that I had taken in that I realized I did not. But one of the things that set me apart from my fellow students was my knowing I had been there before.

Martha King

Interlude at Black Mountain—1956

(with the assistance of Basil King)

Robert Duncan was restless. And hungry. Everyone was.

In the mid-1950s, in North Carolina, a salad was a triangle of iceberg lettuce with a goodly dollop of sweet bright orange "French" dressing from a bottle. Housewives made salads with Jello squares. No one used olive oil. Tiny bottles of olive oil were for sale in Southern drugstores as a laxative or a medicine for burns.

If you don't know of Robert Duncan—in 1956 he was a metaphysical poet entering into his power as a writer and in full possession of his capacity to tell lengthy—very lengthy—stories. Look him up. That fall he had come to teach at Black Mountain College in the mountains of Western North Carolina. The place was remote and underfunded. Western North Carolina was in the middle of bigoted and paranoid mid-century American South. The campus, off a run-down secondary road, was comprised of a hodge-podge of classic Adirondack camp buildings from its former life as a summer camp for children, fleshed out by one-story government surplus prefabs acquired after World War II and interspersed with various modern structures, some large, some lovely, some rickety and unstable, built on the site by students and faculty.

Yes, Robert was hungry. He was restless and a bit trapped. So were others. Intense activity was a norm at Black Mountain, often alone, sometimes in a small group, but there was nothing to do there except work. Except for weekends when there would be an event, a dance, a performance, an exhibit. If one didn't work one might sleep, hang out with others to talk, or ramble off through the mountains along near empty farm roads. Oh yes, there were classes. It was, even in its last days, a school and classes could be the top experience of a day. Or not. We went, or not.

Some classes were communal work events–the doing of weaving, drawing, rehearsing a play. Others, in painting, writing, or composition were public critique with everyone who had new work gathering to talk about what they heard or saw and ask questions about it. The work itself was done alone, in one's studio, just like real life. Charles Olson's classes were famous for marathon workouts: he'd propose an idea that was on his mind and ruthlessly use the students and the time to work through long strings of plausibilities.

A little history: Started in 1933, Black Mountain was conceived as an alternative to normal liberal arts teaching. From the beginning, students were in charge of their own line of study and no one had requirements other than those they chose for themselves.

Yes, Buckminster Fuller came to teach. Annie Albers, Paul Goodman, Josef Albers, Charles Olson, Jacob Lawrence, Willem de Kooning, Franz Kline, John

Cage, Edward Dahlberg, Merce Cunningham, Lou Harrison, M.C. Richards, Stefan Wolpe, Robert Creeley, Peter Voulkous ... and there were many more. But none of these people had famous names at the time. The numbers of students and faculty added together was always very small: 100, 50, 35. And regardless of history or discipline, people there (except for summer institute students) were almost universally low on money as well as marginal in prestige. All were alien to the lives of the mostly poor white farmers in the vicinity, and short of any company but their own and the friends and colleagues who occasionally visited from far away.

Even less famous or honored were the students. Among them, Bob Rauschenberg, Remy Charlip, Arthur Penn, Ed Dorn, John Chamberlain, John Wiencrs, Cy Tombly, Dorothea Rockburne, Basil King. Martha King too but she doesn't figure in this particular tale; this was the fall and she had been there for the summer session only.

All of them, all, were passing in and out of a school committed to freedom in a way hard to imagine today.

Earlier in the school history lights stayed on in the dining hall kitchen 24/7 and intermittently people congregated there. One could scrounge for left-overs from the communal supper, or get coffee from the urn, shoe-leather bitter but a bit stronger than the normal lunch counter brew. Later when the dining hall was closed for economy, kitchens in the cottages where students bunked were also left open to continue the tradition, although coffee had become a treat. The drink was tea, made from bags that were often used three or four times before discard.

On the night of this search, Robert and three painting students were sitting in Robert's apartment at the back of the Studies Building. One of the students claimed that a town 25 miles away had a bus station café with much better food than the bus station in Asheville. Asheville in 1956 had barely moved out of the Great Depression. Boarded-up buildings downtown were minimally interspersed by a Five and Ten, a bus station, a tobacco store, some honky-tonk bars. It was in one of these that Baz (Basil King's nickname) and Eric Weinberger flouted their orthodox Jewish ancestors by ordering and eating pickled pigs feet from the large jar of cloudy grey brine sitting on the counter. Baz said this required a good number of draft beers first. In another of these joints Baz is sure he heard Willie Nelson and Waylon Jennings with their bands. They, like the Black Mountain denizens, were far from famous.

Eating in Asheville pretty much meant the bus station or a diner on Pack Square, Asheville's center that served similar grub. Unless, with a great deal of cash, one could leap up the social scale and dine at the Grove Park Inn, land of white table cloths, high heels, neckties, and luxurious views of blue mountains from the inn's perch above the city. The Asheville Museum had not been dreamed of. Nor the Asheville branch of the University of North Carolina.

There was something hovering over Southern lunch counters in the 1950s. Not only were no customers black, but food that might be "black" was strictly absent.

No hopping John. No spoon bread. No pulled pork. No collards. Sometimes, only sometimes, would a lunch counter have country sausage—hot ground pork full of red and black pepper. And grits. Public food was "American."

The first pizza ever arrived in liberal Chapel Hill late fall 1957, shortly before Martha left for San Francisco. She'd heard it described by a northern friend and couldn't wait to try it but Chapel Hill's students and townsfolk were hesitant and suspicious. By 1957, Black Mountain College was closed and gone. By that time San Francisco was soaring with poetry and New York City roaring with painting and art—but careful behavior ruled in the South. It would be three more years before what was long simmering in the black South emerged for white people to see.

So—a town nearby with a "good" bus station café? Did anyone believe it? They were up for it anyway. The college had a truck for scheduled trips to the town of Black Mountain, five miles away. The only other way out was on foot and the only nighttime destination was a place called Peek's lying on a dirt curve just off the main highway three miles off. Most people walked it both ways. There were six or seven cars among the whole community. Peeks was the only drinking spot anywhere in Buncombe Country, which was Bible Belt bone dry, but then Ma Peeks was the sheriff's cousin and no one said anything about what was served there let alone what went on in the row of small shacks she had out back.

The thought of Peeks was not appealing that night. The idea of getting into a *car* and driving away down the road was. One of the students actually had a car. It was Gray Stone, who had ambled in and joined the group. Lanky taciturn Gray Stone. Everyone thought his parents had a streak of sadism to give him such a first name and everyone always called him by his given and surname run together. He had a car, but no driver's license. It's not clear if he even knew how to drive or how he had gotten the car to the school in the first place but there it was: Grey Stone had an old Chrysler four door. And that night, his obsessive contrarianism notwithstanding, he was generous. He gave Baz the keys and all five of them piled in.

All the way there, Robert talked. He told about living in New York City as a young man. He told them he had been married at the time. He liked his mother-in-law and used to wear her negligee and her pink satin bed jacket and hold forth sitting in bed. He had opinions about everything from Tarot to politics. He said his wife was miffed but his mother-in-law loved it.

Once the group reached the bus station café, Robert told a far longer story. He described a haggard old man whom he had met in New York. The man often came to private uptown affairs where in those deeply closeted days gay men could loosen up and party. The old man was pushed in a wheelchair by a quiet assistant. He was said to be fabulously wealthy. Waving his hands and rolling his wall eye, Robert described a fastidiously dressed, rail-thin person with sunken cheeks, exhausted eyes, and very few teeth. Eventually Duncan had heard his story. A dozen years earlier an ethereally beautiful street kid had turned up making his way in the uptown demimonde. He had disappeared one day with a special patron. He wasn't seen again by anyone. Except that he had been. Sometime after the old man began attending the parties one of the boy's former lovers picked up something–a gesture, a twist of phrase–and pried the story out. Sex with the patron had involved serious beatings, followed every time by lavish gifts of jewels and money. The boy's body went down to ruin, but not before his savings and investments had made him extremely rich.

One of the students said later he was sure he'd read this tale in a book of short stories by Tennessee Williams. Another said that Duncan and Tennessee could have been at the same parties. A third thought Duncan admired the tale and changed the pronouns. In the café no one said anything. Everyone ate. Telling this story in a North Carolina bus station café was its own kind of adventure. Who was hearing this and what would they do? Robert's voice carried on the rhythm of his story-telling was not low or private. It was enthusiastic.

The food turned out to be quite like the diner in Asheville. The thin grey hamburgers, bright orange American cheese, eggs fried in fat. No one made poached or scrambled or soft boiled eggs back then. The counterman cleared the plates as usual and no car full of impromptu defenders of the status quo rolled up to greet the visitors.

They all piled back into the car for the twenty-five miles back, leaving their stomachs to the task of digestion and Baz to negotiate the rattling old car through the miles of dark, mostly empty roads, past houses with lonely lights, through crossroads with shot-up stop signs; all of them just for the moment released.

Tom Patterson

The Convivial Anarchists

Author's note:

The following is a chapter from a memoir-in-the-works about how I spent my twenties. (Working title: Made in the Shade: Cultural Adventures of a Fledgling Writer.*) I spent several of those years as a student at St. Andrews, where the highlight of my academic experience was the 1974 Black Mountain College Festival. Organized to celebrate the avant-garde legacy of the legendary North Carolina school, closed almost 20 years by then, the festival was the brainchild of my mentor professors Whitney Jones and Ron Bayes. After securing nominal support from the St. Andrews administration they raised a few thousand dollars to pay for the project, a series of readings, lectures, panel discussions and exhibitions. It all unfolded over five weeks in February and March, in the final semester of my senior year, and it had a powerful, enduring impact for some of us.*

There were on-campus art exhibitions by Josef Albers and Robert Rauschenberg, and a lineup of speakers, readers and performers, including futurist philosopher Buckminster Fuller, historian Martin Duberman, and poets Robert Creeley, Ed Dorn and Jonathan Williams. All had taught or studied at Black

Mountain except Duberman, who had written a book about the school. As a grand finale to close the festival there was a joint performance by composer John Cage and choreographer Merce Cunningham, who had been frequent visiting artists and teachers at Black Mountain. The following chapter chronicles their arrival in North Carolina for the festival.

"And what is the purpose of writing music? One is, of course, not dealing with purposes but dealing with sounds. Or the answer must take the form of paradox: a purposeful purposelessness or a purposeless play. This play, however, is an affirmation of life--not an attempt to bring order out of chaos, nor to suggest improvements in creation, but simply a way of waking up to the very life we're living, which is so excellent once one gets one's mind and one's desires out of the way and lets it act of its own accord."

–John Cage

On the evening of March fourth, which happened to be my sister Jill's eighth birthday, John Cage and Merce Cunningham flew into the airport outside Fayetteville. Or Fayette-nam, as we called it, alluding to the adjacent military base, Fort Bragg, a training ground for Vietnam-bound troops. I joined Whitney Jones at dusk for the hour-long drive from Laurinburg to pick up the visiting artists. It had rained that afternoon, and there were banks of fog in the low-lying areas we passed through on the drive.

The two avant-garde pioneers were to spend several days at St. Andrews, giving informal talks and presenting the Black Mountain Festival's closing performance. Whitney told me they'd agreed to come for expenses and a cut-rate honorarium of only $500 between the two of them, since they were so enthusiastic about participating in an event honoring Black Mountain College. We were a little late leaving St. Andrews in the college car, an American-made four-door sedan, and we arrived at the airport just in time to meet them as they stepped off the plane. They were a conspicuous odd couple, easy to spot: Slim, tousle-haired Cunningham looked elegant and otherworldly in a gray suit over an open-collared cream-colored sport shirt. Cage—with his broad, squint-eyed grin, bushy gray beard and faded denim outfit—might have been a Sandhills tobacco farmer, except for his unusual shoes, two-toned, lace-up high-tops that appeared to have sewn-on spats.

They seemed to recognize Whitney and me as easily as we did them.

"You're the only people here who look like you're from a college," Cage said, laughing.

In the small airport it took us only a few minutes to retrieve their bags, and soon we were all in the car engaged in friendly conversation while gliding along the blacktop highway, following the headlight beams through intermittently foggy rural countryside. A brief exchange about the fuel shortage and the larger energy crisis led to the subject of Buckminster Fuller, of whom our guests were eager to hear news.

"A marvelous man!" said Cage from the back seat. His voice vaguely reminded me of Vincent Price's.

Whitney and I told them a little about Fuller's recent visit to St. Andrews and the inspiring lecture he'd given. Cunningham, sitting alongside Cage, started reminiscing about their adventures with Bucky at Black

Mountain. Cage remembered an old Model A Ford Bucky regularly drove in those years. "It got good gas mileage," he said, speaking of the energy crisis. They recalled the obscure Erik Satie play they'd worked on together at Black Mountain in 1948, *The Ruse of Medusa*, translated by their friend M.C. Richards. The production starred Bucky, Cunningham and Elaine De Kooning, among others, with sets designed by Willem De Kooning. And Cage, of course, as musical director. It was directed by Arthur Penn, whose breakthrough moment would come 20 years later with his film *Bonnie and Clyde*. Cunningham remembered the enterprise as great fun, and said he mentioned it because it transformed Bucky's way of presenting himself in his public lectures, leading him to become more of a showman. They were amused when I told them about the gyroscope demonstration he'd performed to illustrate the twelve degrees of freedom, when he got all wound up in his microphone cord.

As Whitney drove us slowly through the little town of Maxton, Cage and Cunningham peered attentively out the windows and commented on details that stood out in the light from the overhead street lamps and storefront fixtures. Cage asked if I was related to the Pattersons whose last name was engraved in stone over the door of a brick building from the late 19th century. Not that I knew of, I told him. This led into a brief exchange of information about our family backgrounds and places of origin. They seemed very intrigued by the information Whitney shared with them about the Lumbee Indians, who made up much of the population in Maxton and the larger Sandhills region—believed by some to be descended from the legendary Lost Colony. Even though our visiting artists regularly traveled the world, they seemed completely engaged with and genuinely interested in everything about this remote, thinly populated stretch of North Carolina.

The dazzling science-fiction lights of a new plate-glass factory on Laurinburg's eastern outskirts glowed through the fog-shrouded swamp we passed near the end of our ride. We found St. Andrews also lit up but not quite so brightly. The nocturnal view of Lake Ansley Moore drew exclamations from the back seat as we crossed the dam separating the lake from a cypress swamp at one end of the campus.

"It looks like the lake at Black Mountain," Cage remarked.

Our immediate destination was the big, brand-new auditorium at Scotland County High School, where Bucky Fuller had lectured a few weeks earlier. There we met up with theatre professor Dub Narramore and two of his students. As we all gathered on the stage where Cage and Cunningham were to perform the following evening, Whitney cleared his throat and nervously eyed the special guests. Then he apologized in advance for delivering some information he'd only received that afternoon: The high-school administration had scheduled another event in the auditorium lobby the following evening at the same time Cunningham and Cage were to be performing inside. This other event—an employees' banquet dinner for a local power-tool plant—was set to run from 7:00 to 9:00 p.m. The performance was to begin at 8:00 p.m. Apparently the people in charge of the building saw no conflict in the simultaneous bookings, since they would be in separate rooms.

Whitney paused for a moment to let the news sink in. "I wanted you to see the auditorium before I told you," he went on, explaining that it had been booked for the performance because the largest auditorium at the college was too small to accommodate the numbers of people expected to attend. There was, in effect, no other option. Furthermore, Whitney explained, because the audience would be unable to enter and exit the high-school auditorium through the lobby, they would have to be routed through the exits on either side of the stage. He said that he'd been horrified to find out about the scheduling conflict at the eleventh hour.

The unspoken concern, of course, was that Cage and Cunningham might refuse to perform. But after Whitney finished explaining the situation, they seemed completely unperturbed. Cage just smiled, gestured toward the lobby and said, "Outside there will be food, and inside there will be food for thought."

Everyone laughed. Nothing else was said about it, and we moved on to discuss plans for the performance. Cunningham noted that the stage floor was varnished— not so great for dancing, but he would manage, he said. The program was to be billed as a "Dialogue," during which he would perform a series of solo dances while Cage provided a sound component with no relationship to the dances except that it would be going on in the same place at the same time.

Cage wondered aloud about the room's acoustics and walked backstage for a moment to inspect the in-house grand piano. It would need to be rolled onstage for his closing piano solo, he explained. While the audience looked on, he would "prepare" the piano by placing rubber clamps and screws on some of the strings. Then he would take a seat and play the piece, titled *Music for Marcel Duchamp*, which he'd composed in 1947, shortly before he and Cunningham went to teach and perform at Black Mountain for the first time.

I stood by quietly observing and listening, awed that they'd been close friends of Duchamp, a personal favorite even then, when I knew little about art. And of course awed by the fact that I was standing on a stage with John Cage and Merce Cunningham.

Prior to the piano piece, Cage went on to explain, his time onstage would be spent reading a much longer, spoken-word composition called "Empty Words," derived from Thoreau's Journals. For this he would need a chair, a small table, a reading lamp, a microphone, two slide projectors and a slide screen. He'd brought slide reproductions of Thoreau's simple drawings, also from the Journals, to be projected onto a screen situated above him as he read. The projectors—which Whitney confirmed could be borrowed from the college's AV department—could rest on the stage floor near the orchestra stairs on the left side, where someone could be unobtrusively stationed to operate them.

Without a second thought I promptly volunteered for the job. Cage said there would be a timed score for the slides and promised to go over it with me the next day. He borrowed my notebook long enough to sit in one of the audience seats and, in his distinctive, calligraphic script, write down brief information about the music, to be included in a program handed out to audience members. Taking a seat beside him, Cunningham added an additional note about the dances he planned to perform—solos from longer ensemble pieces whose titles he listed. Cage made a few copy-editing changes and drew a curving arrow to indicate that the information on the dances should appear first. Then he handed the notebook back to me, and I volunteered to arrange for the programs to be printed. At this point, seizing an obvious opportunity, I spontaneously decided to blow off my classes for the next day in order hang out with the visiting artists. I offered to fetch them from their hotel, take them out for lunch, then bring them back to the auditorium and help them set everything up.

Not until we were leaving the auditorium did Cage casually mention that they hadn't had dinner. It was almost 10:00 p.m., and most Laurinburg dining establishments had closed for the night. While Whitney drove us to the nearby Holiday Inn, where our guests would be lodging, he and I discussed the matter. At the front desk the two late-arriving travelers checked in and got their room keys, then we took their minimal luggage to their adjoining rooms. Cunningham settled in while Cage, Whitney and I went off to search for a takeout restaurant still serving customers. We were thrilled to discover the Pizza Inn still open. When we entered I recognized the girl at the cash register as a St. Andrews student, although I didn't know her name. She smiled at us, then called out to alert someone in the back that we were there. A guy in a bright red uniform shirt emerged from the kitchen, and she stage-whispered to him, "That's John Cage."

The kitchen guy was a "townie," and looked like the good-ol'-boy, type—not likely to be familiar with Cage or any other contemporary experimental composer. He was accommodating in any case, and seemed to understand that the bearded gentleman in the farmer's jacket was someone special. Cage quickly perused a menu, then inquired about an item not on it, namely steak. The guy disappeared into the kitchen for a moment, then returned with an open box of raw steaks that he presented for Cage's inspection.

"We only bring these out for important people like the President," he said. Cage smiled broadly, looked at the steaks, thought for a moment, and then said he would have a pizza after all. When he specified sausage and jalapeño peppers, the good-ol'-boy said, "Oh, you don't want that!" He insisted the peppers were too hot to eat, but Cage wasn't to be dissuaded. While the pizza was in the works, we walked to a nearby convenience store, where Cage bought two Miller beers, a bottle of red wine, and a head of lettuce. Then we returned to the Pizza Inn and claimed the too-hot pizza. As we were climbing back into the car I noticed a dime on the asphalt and picked it up.

The exchange about the jalapeño peppers reminded Cage of a story involving his Aunt Marge, which he recounted as Whitney drove us back to the Holiday Inn. When Cage's recording of his retrospective performance at New York's Town Hall was released, Aunt Marge placed a special order for it at her local music store. When she went in to purchase the album, the sales clerk said, "Are you sure you want to buy this?" He pointed out that it was a five-record boxed set costing

$25. "Well, in that case, I don't want it," Aunt Marge said to the clerk. We all erupted in laughter.

Thinking about his Aunt Marge, Cage recalled an occasion when she quietly confided her feelings about a new washing machine: "You know, I love this washing machine much more than I love your Uncle Walter." Uncle Walter, Cage added, was a terrible man who forbade Aunt Marge's singing in the church choir; he said it kept her from her housework. "She had a lovely contralto voice and used to sing with choirs before she married him. But after Uncle Walter died, Aunt Marge turned him into a veritable saint. She wouldn't allow anyone to say anything against him."

As Whitney steered into the parking lot in front of the Holiday Inn, I promised Cage I'd be back to pick them up shortly before noon the next day.

"I have to think of an easy way to remember your names tomorrow," Cage said as he was getting out of the car. "You're Whitney, so I'll think of the Whitney Museum in New York. And you're Tom Patterson, so I'll associate you with William Carlos Williams' Paterson."

As we drove away he remained standing in front of the Holiday Inn with his pizza box and his bag of groceries in one arm, waving at us with the other. In the greenish glow given off by the parking-lot lights, I could see that infectious grin still on his face.

Whitney drove out of the parking lot and slowed the car to a stop as he clicked on his turn signal before entering the highway. Then we looked at each other and simultaneously burst out laughing.

Peter McNamara

A Flight of Terns

such and such (to the nth degree)
its distress slashed across the sky
the assault of scents on sense—
stealthy, febrile, intrepid—why
ought orange be the garb of truth
Chesterton's old chestnut queried
to our age of Darwinian doubt

lime yellow etched in bas relief
beneath that conjured elm shade
we've never ceased to yearn for:
so *there* ... now where (away) ...
sun splinters detonate glare on
what we look to shelter, so seek
to deflect ... to no avail where
it determines to ferret us out, as

in nightsweats murk tunnels deep
in muck, ash-ground slag ... one
can scarcely go on ... enervated
unnerved despite intent ... then
a breeze sweeps through and all
is digitized ... reimaged (merely)
a flight of terns drops in to roost
reconfiguring (to a new default)
whew! thank fortune for that!
beware the thurifer amid clouds
of incense irresolute to sanctify

Cross Currents

Shards of light are absorbed, swallowed by
birches; susurrus stirs spent corn stalks
like rumor presaging revolt. Down-meadow
Holsteins, through a break in the wire, stray
flummoxed beneath low-dipping maples.
A stallion shoulders pasture's dapple, marks
time as does the shadow-shifting-steeple.

Complacence undoes so many:
blithe along fairways with no sense of irony's
cross currents skewing life's plumb off true,
scrambling songbirds' GPS through lapses
in the magnetic field.

You get to where you know
you aren't getting anywhere, time's bounty
scarcer, its cost dearer. The sun, no longer
bothering to set, meanders off, entering and
exiting to inexplicable cues.

Will the Rapture catch us up?
Or will we end in urns on unknown mantels?
A few bolder voices renounce the party line,
the volatility index spikes, and making par
becomes a heroic feat. Maples' scarlet/
gold—in gyres—snatch at life's up-swirl
pulses still urgent in their stems and veins.

Underground

Mining the subway, its serpentine
white-tiled halls alive with echoes
at junctions east-with-west and at
turnings the jewel for eye or ear
come upon, sprung up—sprouts
of would-be art from some failed
Julliard tyro—visual, visceral—

The Underground (as Brits
say) half-life pulsing, hidden by
happenstance (or intent), gallery
for Peter Lorre's *M,* unsettling
spills of garish light rousing the
fantastic. Here (always) are tonals
yet to become light: late Rothko.

And somewhere sun stirs water
to wildfire igniting tongues—gilt
engulfing furrows, candling caps.
Here it's mad as a run-down dog
or as fitful as cloaked Caravaggio
shrinking from guilty memories.

Aubergine

A hint of Pernod in the Oysters Rockefeller
the breaching & sounding of whales in heat
green fantailing off a proximate mountain
and hard bodies awash under a bright sun
anchor disparate nuances in the constricted
landscape. Shimmers of early June pulse
through our age of manufactured heroes, its
conveyer belt of platitudes and euphemisms
so unrelenting as to shatter our equanimity.
Yet savory breezes—Gallic, anise—scour
the mind, clear it of conflicting tincts and
float, as it then is, a freshened clarity on air.

The otherness of aubergine, its fathomless
Reddish purple/brown in changing light
midnight blue, black or red—none of these
—its seed spilling into the sluggish life stream.
Oracles probe isobars amid foodstuffs for an
out-of-season Black Friday; élan of the poet
in sharp-shouldered tweed launching dash
against recitation's purple air; a sprinkle of
sycophancy radiates warmth at his reception
as life flakes like old paint from a cream-gold
staircase, retention—intent—a step or two
behind, hope—elusive, evanescent in the
intense sunlight—its cobwebbed chimera.

Whit Griffin

from *The Universal Lyre*

             The glorification   of Enoch.
Carna, mother of alphabetical letters.
                              Hugh Plat
        invented
             alphabet blocks and
                         the turn-spit;
secret inks   and a method of penmanship.
             Dionysus writes speeches
                         for Coriolanus.
        Martinez de Pasqually's   2400 names
Six books   on the plagiarisms   of   Menander.

        Menander's

        posthumous glory.
        Menander wrote over one hundred plays
though few were deemed successful in his lifetime.
             Posterity lionized his name,
                         and a statue was erected
in the Theatre of Dionysus at Athens.

Am I to be sold?
        Have I been poisoned?
                 Am I to be reconciled with my offspring?
                 Is he who left home still alive?

        *

Beliefs the brain has about the body.

Manipulating the experience
of having a body. Which Orisha claims your head?
The idea
that blood is sea water
infused with fire.

The idea
that blood and salt
are magical equivalents because they taste alike.
Nicolas Cusa claimed
the blood of Germans was not
the same weight as that of Italians.

As Italy to Saturnia.   The tooth of Saturn.
The castration of Ra.
The gospel of castration.
Lazarus and Barefoot Cyril wandered through Bulgaria
preaching the virtues of nakedness and
self-emasculation.   The last Chinese eunuch
died in 1996.
Both Attis and Mars were said
to be conceived on March 25.

Attis was born of a virgin,
who swallowed an almond.

Juno Februata, virgin mother of Mars.

As December 24 is the Night of the Mother.

The Trojans built an altar
to Aphrodite in Sicily.
The Neolithic shrine to Astarte at Byblos.
Islam offended the Great Goddess so she cursed Arabia
and departed.

*

       The deluge acts as a wave of translation.
Born of the Ninefold
Sea-goddess and cast
     ashore on the ninth wave.
            The threefold moon.
     The goddess of exhaustion who is also
           one of the moon's phases.

For generations the Sawney Bean family
     lived on human flesh.
   But few men know on what Valhalla's
champions feed.
A pregnant woman is encouraged
       to eat quinces and coriander seed.

         Loki is beaten in an eating
   contest. Seth is allowed three glances into
   the Garden of Eden.
   Wisdom is gained with the loss of eyesight.
As it is said
   Tiresias received his prophetic powers
by becoming a woman and living as a temple harlot
     for seven years. Fintan, the salmon
caught by Fionn.
     Fenris swallows the sun.
The legend that says Pilate was born beneath
   the Fortingall yew.

The idea of Christianity
emerged from the yew tree.

  *

On this cross-tree hung apples
that were symbols of the divine
essence that had produced humankind.

The essence   of   five trees.

        Attis was sacrificed on a pine tree. At Hierapolis,

      victims of Artemis
              were hung on artificial trees

      in her temple. The Mead Tree
              is the source of unborn souls.
Consus,
the god who presides over secret councils.
        The god of agriculture who symbolizes
the secret processes of nature.
      At the harvest festival
               held in his honor
horses and mules were crowned with flowers and given
a holiday. Rosemary
            to crown the boar's head.
The lucky swine swallows the henbane.
      Sygbert was stabbed by a swineherd. Boars for
Astarte
              and Demeter.
Until we stop killing the animals we won't stop killing
each other.

Astarte rules the spirits of the dead
             in heaven.
      A cemetery of crocodiles
          at Tebtunis.
Anubis possessed the knowledge of embalming.
      Through an act of surrender Odin discovered
the runes. One-eyed Odin,
      a phallic god. Some say Athena's Palladium

was a lingam.
Gilded genitals
in Cybele's bridal chamber.

Azazel hails from Syria bearing a message.
The Syrians had their violet petal sherbet.

The Assyrian royal household had an unbroken
line of succession for a thousand years.

Minos composed his laws in a holy
cave in the Dictaean mountain,
and claimed he had received them
from Zeus.

Baal-Gad, the Semitic Pan, was worshipped
in a cave at the source of the Jordan.

For to the Arcadians Pan is the most ancient
and the most honoured of all the gods.

Baal to Bel to Balder. The Celts consecrated
henbane to Belenus, the god of oracles
and the sun.

Joseph Bathanti

My Mother and Father

Eight stout bales of coiled hay
since first threshing, May–

three, maybe four, years ago–
lay at the edge of the swales,

somehow forgotten by the folks
who lease Billings' dogleg,

and tend tobacco that glows,
come harvest, as if the sun bled

the plowsoles. This morning
the monarch bides the lavender thistle-

down, wings opening, closing,
marking time in its imaginal phase,

dispersing eggs among the last autumn flowers.
On the creek bank, deer grind

green husks, hulls like shark skin,
the ancient Chestnut drops.

Their cuneiform prints fork the silt
left from August flash floods.

The fog is shot with blue-gray beams,
gauzy breast a portal to everlasting.

Strangers walk here,
with their burdens and assignations.

They read the writing spiders' ideograms,
legible at first light, rimed in dew—

in seconds, deliquesced.
Webs cup the Rose of Sharon.

Those two lone cedars in the gap:
my mother and father.

Thomas Meyer

"A Rhapsody" from *Porcelain Pillow*

What isn't thought, pointed at, counted, or tripped over is a word

*Let us go & gather blue lotuses nonchalant, a hand
in the water trailing*

*Et par le pouvoir d'un mot
Je recommence ma vie
Je suis né pour te connaître
Pour te nommer*

*We've just begun to
see, to know how lucky we are*

In my *Book of Memory*, in the early part where there is little to be read, there comes a chapter with the heading: *Incipit vita nova*. It is my intention to make this little book from the words I find written under that selection— if not all of them, at least the essence of their meaning.

Un petit garcon sur la plage. French cobbled together to describe my shirt, one bought to wear to the gym but now for street wear. Too stylish really to hide among the exercise equipment. White with rainbow trim, chic detailing. How I long to speak another language. Such a surprise that I don't. If not pressed, at the table, I can fake French. In Germany my not speaking the language is taken as some sort of stealth. Never got Spanish despite three classroom years. Ditto Russian, even longer exposure in high school. Did speak Plattdeutsch as a child, three or four years old. My grandmother felt English was much too difficult a language for children.

Never having been thrown into the panic and necessity of immersion, maybe that's why. But it's just as much, if not more, a matter of self-consciousness. No talent, skill, or inclination is mine when it comes to singing, throwing a ball, or dancing in public. Odd physical self-consciousness, especially because I've never been squeamish about nakedness. Maybe such things are more complicated than they seem. Or much less.

In my dreams appear people from my waking life, present and past. But they bear no physical likeness to their diurnal counterparts. As though my history were a play being cast and performed by an amateur theater company where there's no consideration being given to the original characters' resemblances. This experience brings with it an uncanny distance from myself. And relief.

Moon, pale and bleary-eyed,
Not able to sleep at night?
Or stay awake each day?
Are you as much in love
As I am?

Jonathan Greene

Halloween Mask

An upside-down paper sack
with slits for the eyes,

anonymous, pretending
to be an unknown entity.

At play through this artifice,
the world changed

and ever after I was always
looking out of the dark,

bewildered by
the world of grown-ups.

Where the House Stood

The house fell in.
Time's a slow bomb.

The plans once
made in the kitchen
leaked out the cook stove
chimney.

All the warmth
of the bedroom
sucked into the cold
endless space of stars.

The world's memory—
so highly selective
and haphazard.

Homage

Every street you wander,
carrying your family tree with you,
down to your toes, roots
looking for an earth to scratch in.

You thank your ancestors
for so much. Then stub your big toe
on some malady they passed on.
Encoded as it is.

You are their whole package.
By chance. Entrusted.
Good and bad.

And without thinking,
add some small increment
all your own.

Your

rootstock
I grafted
onto

flowered
bore fruit
flourished

separation
no
option

Comfort

My hand
on your back,
yours on mine
—sensual as always

but with less
electricity,
more
poultice.

Decades of knowing
each other's touch.
Presences
we go on

By Chance

So few things saved.

Almost all of History
is Retrospect.

Posterity stops
counting losses.

Almost all eyes are glued
to Today, forecasts for
unknowable Futures.

Forgotten: all those gaudy colors
from the statues of Antiquity.

Simon Perchik

Simon Perchik

*

This rock no longer tries
though you give each grave
the tool it needs

—does it matter
you haven't looked here in years
—you bring the dead

and your forehead each day
closer to the ground
easy to grab, hold close

let it harden, already
scraped for the powder
that cures, can stop the breathing.

*

With your mouth closed
swallow though this rain
is already rain and further on

—you have a taste for darkness
fill your belly the way the Earth
each night escapes as a small hole

clings to one hillside
carried by another—you become
its grave, eat without fingers

without knees or the headlong dive
this dirt is used to, held down
and looking for more rain

for shoreline starting out
not yet a whisper, lost
cleared away and for your lips.

*

Every wall has a resting place
kept warm though in the dark
it drains, overgrown with cracks

and grasses: you brush on footpaths
the way every greenhouse is nourished
heated by the mouth on your mouth

—another coat seems reasonable
so you paint this wall over and over
till what's left standing overflows

never dries into that slow love song
from before the sun grew huge
it would fit into this room, had time

to stay and night not yet surrounded
falling behind, from far away
weeping into nothing at all.

*

This rain has no moisture left, falls
as the light from bells
struck from behind

the way all hillsides
are hollowed out for stars
no brighter than this grass

though these graves never know
where next, they listen
for pieces, reminded

by how the first sun
broke apart—they hear it
in the dried-up warmth

for which your shadow is made
—what they hear
no longer remembers

your heart was where
it was safe
and before your heart

waves that started its cry
toward the second sun
and then another, then another

and yet this rain comes back
even without a sky
comes as in the beginning

in splendor, not yet a morning
on the over and over thirst
still not allowed in the open.

*

Empty and the sand
follows you along Broadway
as if some dampness

was left for shoreline
moves the IRT up
then down the way clammers

use their feet to rake
—you walk on tracks
careful not to miss

while the train underneath
breaks open its doors
all at once—no, you don't jump

nothing like that
—these shells are the same
the mad feel for

though their sweat takes the place
water grieves into
and their mouths are the same

let you yell down
and not a mark inside your body
to call you by.

John "Jomo" Williamson

Couple

No two divorces are alike. Some are dramatic—full of sound and fury—and some are so quiet that the news travels slowly, if at all. "Oh, did you know....?" someone asks in a parking lot, at church, or coming out of the bank. "I haven't heard the reasons, but, anyway, maybe it was money or...." and the purveyor lowers his or her eyelids a bit and looks away with a shake of the head.

But, no matter, the mystery of it is always deeper than that attending marriage, since unhappiness is so complex, so particular to a given situation.

When some close friends of mine decided to build a new house, they bought a lot out in the country and planted a couple of trees on it. The house when it was completed was beautiful—and it still is—spacious, and decorated with taste and delicacy. There were parties, and family gatherings, and in the summer, long evenings on the wraparound front porch that looked out over a lake and a forest.

My friends had been together for thirty years—their children were grown and moved away, and the house was quite large for two people, but there's something to be said for space, for the sense of freedom it gives as you drift from room to room on a rainy day and then lie down for a bit in the guest room, looking out the window you never really looked out before as the rain splashes on the glass, smearing the outlines of the trees and other houses.

But the realization that something had been irrevocably wrong came to me much later, months after I'd heard that they'd separated and would divorce. I thought of one spring day when I'd stopped by and my friends were outside working on the front lawn. The grass had been cut and they were weeding the flower beds that ran to either side of the walkway. Lewis—I'd known him a few years longer than Angie—had a new camera—he'd shown it to me before—and he'd been taking pictures around the yard.

"Look at this," he said and turned the camera toward me so I could see the little display screen on the back. Inside the open throat of a lily, two little green frogs with red eyes were entwined around each other, looking directly at the viewer.

"Wow," I said and turned to Angie, who was about twenty feet away, weeding around one of the trees,

"Y'all should frame this and put it in with the family portraits."

She nodded. "It's cute." Then she went back to weeding.

I looked at Lewis. He was still holding the camera up for me to see the picture of the frogs and he looked at me closely. Then he let his hand drop and he put the camera on a little table with some shears and gloves and a glass of ice water.

"I got lucky," he said, reaching for the shears. "You only get one chance for a shot like that."

Ocean View

I often dream of houses—usually old ones. In my dreams, I'm trying to understand why the hallways or staircases no longer lead to a specific room that I'm looking for—I guess because the houses I'm dreaming of are based on memories of houses I've lived in or maybe even the one I'm living in now. The neighborhoods around the houses are different, too and more often than not, when I walk outside, I'm either lost or confused. But in all of these dreams, while I may be disoriented, I'm never scared. I just seem to wander, looking for something.

About ten years ago, when I first began to dream about houses, I had a recurring dream about a certain house. It was white and old-fashioned, like a dream home from a children's book in the 1930s. Impossibly, it sat on a little dune on the oceanfront with the front door facing the ocean. When I would go inside, all manner of friends and relatives would be moving among the rooms, sometimes living there, sometimes just visiting. And while the rooms were spacious and had furniture in them, there were no windows—or the windows were heavily curtained.

But this was ten years ago and the house and the people occupying it seemed to disappear from my dreams—until last week, when one night I dreamed of the white house again. This time, I could make out a bit more of it, but only from the outside. There was a little roof over the front door, supported by two ornate wooden brackets. I was walking on the beach and looked up at it, and lights were on in the rooms and the curtains were open and people were moving in the rooms. I walked up to the front door and walked in—and then I woke up.

My wife and I live alone now. Our children have grown up and left our house, although they come home to visit from time to time. And our house is quite large, much larger than we need, so, with that thought in mind, we'll sometimes drive around looking at neighborhoods where we might like to re-locate.

Last Sunday we took a drive out to Norfolk, and ended up in Ocean View, a neighborhood that sweeps along the Chesapeake Bay until it ends at Willoughby Spit, a peninsula created by a hurricane in the late 1600s. We stopped at a restaurant at First View and had lunch. The restaurant has a large deck overlooking the ocean. Off to the west, the arc of Willoughby Spit, like all of Ocean View that fronts the water, is embedded with bungalows that poke above the small dunes separating them from the beach. Most of these homes are fairly new, but some are old and date back to the early 1900s when Ocean View first became a tourist destination.

We finished lunch and drove farther west until there was only one right turn remaining to go over to the beach, so we took it, planning to park the car and walk out to the water. My wife was driving and she turned right and then left into the final street. After about one hundred feet, I looked out my window and the white house in my dreams was directly in front of me.

"Stop, could you?" I said, trying to keep my voice steady, for a moment not sure if what I was seeing was real or if, for just that moment, I was dreaming. "It's that house."

My wife put on the brakes, looking out the rear window and then at me. "What are you talking about?"

"That place there. It's so old." I couldn't bring myself to say that I'd dreamed about it, because, had I? Wasn't it just a coincidence?

She pulled into the driveway opposite and turned the car around. Now the house was on her side. We drove slowly past and then we turned onto Fifteenth View and she parked the car. We got out and walked along the planked pathway out to the beach and then continued for a while until the rear of the house was in clear view. Under a second floor porch was a door that opened onto a small concrete deck.

It's like a front door, I thought, but didn't say anything.

We walked along the beach for a while, tossing some pebbles into the water and watching the traffic roar across the bridge over to Hampton. Then we turned around and walked back the way we had come, passing the back of the house again. In an open window on the second floor, someone—I couldn't tell if it was a man or a woman—was silhouetted for a moment, and then drew a curtain across the window. Then I looked to the first floor—it couldn't have been more than a few seconds later—and the same thing happened: someone stood for a moment at the window and then drew the curtain.

"Did you see that?" I touched my wife's arm.

She was looking out over the ocean but turned and looked at me.

"Not really." She looked past me at the house. "Something to do with that?" she shifted her glance toward the house.

"Yes." I shrugged. "Anyway..." my voice tailed off.

When we got back to our car I said, "Do you want me to drive back?"

She nodded and I got in the driver's seat. Then I pulled out of the parking space and drove down the street to take one last look. To either side of the front door were two windows and as I drove past someone drew the curtains across the window to the left of the door.

"Did you see that?" my wife said.

I turned into the same driveway she had used earlier to turn around, and I backed out and drove slowly past. I didn't look at the house again.

"No," I said, "what was it?"

We looked at each other as I turned right on Fifteenth View out to Ocean View Avenue and paused at the stop sign.

"When we drove past just now, someone was standing in one of the upstairs windows," she said.

I pulled out onto the Avenue and began driving east.

"Was it a man or a woman?

She coughed and then picked up a can of Pepsi she'd been drinking. "Oh, it was a man." She took a sip. "But he was dressed in an old suit—you know—the kind with big lapels and he had one of those old hats on ... um, a fedora, I think they call it."

I nodded.

"Anyway," she said as she put the Pepsi can back, "it was an interesting house, especially that little roof over the front door. You just don't see those kind of brackets anymore, do you?"

Twilight

She wasn't much different from most girls her age, maybe a bit taller, paid a bit less attention to her clothing and makeup, but the essentials were there. And I remember passing her in the hallway once in the middle of the winter and she smelled like spring—not the scent of flowers, but the clear clean smell of rain and earth that drifts up to you as you stand at the edge of a plowed field some morning in early March.

I'm old now and I was old when she was my World Literature student; there was at least forty years difference in our ages, but I often found myself wondering if she accepted the positions I took, if my opinions had any relevance to her, if, in other words, she was attracted to me in a way that precluded what was so different about us.

And I don't mean this simply in an academic way. Certainly, some of my comments in class were amusing, or off-putting, or even silly at times—but how did they strike *her*? What in the glances she would send me or the comments she would make created a distinct connection between us?

And so I found myself acceding a bit to her flourishes in class, her absurd little statements and desire to be noticed. At times, I would toss something off and she'd catch the idea and run with it—only to run it into the ground. But I let her do that. And often, I'd wonder if the other students noticed— if they thought that perhaps

I'd given her a license they were denied. But, of course, none of them ever let on.

The time for final papers eventually came, and with it, conferences with each student. Allotted no more than ten minutes to outline their individual research questions, they listened as I dissected their ideas—accepted some, had them rethink others – and sent them on their way. When it was her turn, she sat down quickly, opened her notebook to a page of rather sloppy notes and glanced at me.

"I've got a couple of ideas." She said and then looked at me closely.

"OK." I glanced over at her notes, then at her. She was wearing a white cotton blouse, open at the throat.

"But I just can't make up my mind."

I nodded but tried not to look at her directly, as if my eyes would betray something I didn't want her to see. But after a few minutes, she focused on a topic and I said, "Sounds good."

She stood up and looked down at me. She was a tall girl and her brown hair was long and cascaded over her shoulders.

"There's something I want to tell you," she said as she gathered up her things.

I felt the breath catch in my throat and I turned away for a moment to look out the classroom window at the early evening.

"What's that?" I said and looked up at her.

"You remind me of someone—but I don't know how to pronounce the name—Akenback?"

She was smiling, as if secretly amused at something only she understood.

"He's the guy in *Death in Venice*. You know..."

"Aschenbach?" I said.

She nodded. "Yeah, him."

"Oh?" I caught myself blushing a bit. "Why's that?"

She was at the door now, about to turn and leave the classroom.

"But you should know," she said, dropping her eyes to look at something in her purse. She shook her head and then looked back at me.

"Remember? You told us that he was looking for something the world wouldn't let him have even if he could get it."

"I said that?" I shrugged. "Well, I guess there are lots of interpretations—"

She shook her head again. "No, you were right. I read that story a couple of times. That's why I wanted to mention it now." She smiled.

"I guess we're all looking for some meaning in life, aren't we?" I said and looked at her.

"Sure...that's what it is, but—"She paused. "I guess there really *is* the impossible, though—like you said."

I nodded and looked down for a moment. Then I looked up. She was staring at me.

"Aschenbach had achieved all the 'possibles,' you know?" I looked away for a moment. "That was his error—men are not gods."

She was still staring at me, but a smile had crossed her face.

"But he didn't know that, did he?"

I looked up at her.

"No, I guess he didn't."

"Well, then, *Herr Doktor,*" she said and laughed, "I'll see you later." And she turned and left the room.

By now, the darkness outside was complete—and I stood up, watching my reflection in the glass as I walked over to the windows and looked out to where the lights from the opposite bank were shimmering on the river.

Dick Bakken

Aboriginal Elegy

Sung soprano by a mother,
the close family lowing deep mortal
sighs, grunt chorus and shout
from communal circle of a tribe

brown cow gold cow
lowing with their bells loud
[uh-hah uh-hoh, uh-hah uh-hoh]
moo moo uh! oh! my echo

day star go down
gopher in the deep ground
[uh-hah uh-hoh, uh-hah uh-hoh]
moo moo uh! oh! my echo

red ants white gown
whirring with a blood sound
[uh-hah uh-hoh, uh-hah uh-hoh]
moo moo uh! oh! my echo

my son way down
laughing in the dead mound
[uh-hah uh-hoh, uh-hah uh-hoh]
moo moo uh! oh! my echo

whoop!   whoop! whoop!

cheecha doom, cheecha doom, doom doom
cheecha doom, cheecha doom, doom doom

whoop!

[uh-hah uh-hoh, uh-hah uh-hoh]

whoop! whoop!

Wrested from Betst

Lines 3–4 are from Elizabeth Thornton's
"With Special Thanks to Natt N. Dodge"

Yes! wrest my dress to this floor
frothing us rabidly

my love,
my back-fanged snake, my kissing bug

sidewind me hard, whiskered
raw, plunge against these sucked ring-torn ears,

my fists
pounding loud as our hearts through all

wasted thorny Sonora ...
scrawling

this sky down upon us, slamming against floorboards,
unrhymed sidewise flashes, burst bang-bright

thunder of bliss, our own scorching mirage, horrid
toxic mosquito haze to hurl us

around like spooked
javalina blundered into crashed chairs

under this table
our voltage-fevered lightning-slash deluge, frenzy booms,

boiling swarms of eye-bite no-see-ums, glorious
crawling nightshade swooped by kamikaze bats, black, whizzed

like dum-dums ripping past—
Damn rat-a-tat bloated border enforcers

vaulting in Bermuda shorts and halter tops from fold-ups
to pepper this venomous butt-edge of America

as we gasp enrapturing out our flaming sunset *finito*,
a sharp fury raged cry.

Silvery Branches

19ʰ Annual Watershed Eco-Poetry Festival,
Civic Center Park, Berkeley, Sept. 27, 2014

Into our dark forest
trots the spirit, white and bushy.
His loves are laughing after him in such
striped sweaters and mittens.
This spirit carries the axe in his teeth
but nothing yet on the lupine slope
of his spine. O it is snowing so brightly
and soft. For it is our season
of joy and singing
together before that night when
even the flying deer bound down in love
to choose from dreamy faces
who will ride
and who will open again
into daybreak with their whistling
wings alighting in every swirl of tree.
This one!
says the girl.
Calls the boy *Ree! Here!*
grasps the axe from sparkled
teeth of the wolf.
Remus, this will be ours for the tapers
and bells, for the gifts strewn under O!
all around. You will ferry
it as we carol back to the little

home. And he straps a youngest spruce
to this spirit's back, slips that axe
into the teeth.

Brenda Butka

Morning Service on 21st

This alley my cathedral,
running west to east,
classical, unadorned,
one side chapel Peabody's Shoe Repair,
boots bending in their glass boxes,
cupola slowly gathering
its daily increment of sky.

A boy in a black apron
leans, slack, against the wall,
its intricate mosaic
old brick and peeling paint,
smoking. His cigarette unfurls
its blue incense into the air.
Doves confess their sins,
murmuring straight into the ear of god.

The sun staggers up behind the bookstore
roaring
like resurrection.
We have survived.
We have our own regrets.
It's a new day, not
so bad, new, and
we praise it.

Daytrippers

They roll rubber-tired carts
down to the beach, sit
on chairs made of plastic ribbons,
bright in the shifting dark
under the pier,
its bolted posts and crossbeams a little forest
of striped shade.

A tidy old man, checkered skin
loose at the neck, skims the sand
for treasure, sends a little boy wild
with unimaginable antiquity—
a rusted penny, 1984.

His wife talks to her friend
about when women wore mink stoles
to the movies in Raleigh and Fayetteville.

Sea oats shiver in the heat,
chime silently on the dunes.
Yep. A hundred and four inland. Hot.
Kicking his 4-wheeler, the beach patrol
disappears into the light, exhaust
boiling behind.

Bony elbows angular as katydids,
the kids skitter like sanderlings in the foam,
hunch under sunhats,
sensibly digging a hole to China
with a red plastic shovel.
Young girls with their round arms
toss their hair. Boys, uneasy, stare.

Petulant at the end of the day,
children wrapped in towels
like striped shrouds
turn towards home,
the sun a palm of blessing,
bright oil streaming down,
the sea still murmuring
its customary psalm.

Dibba

The pond was Dibba's place,
her mark everywhere.
Old Dad in Laurinburg with young Tom and Helen,
and Maxton where Clarkie Belle
ruled the shadowed house.

Johns Pond was in between, her own place.
We walked through her garden to the pier:
forsythia's yellow exclamations, trumpet vine
yaupon holly. She planted yucca, henon bamboo,
windmill palms, but she knew them all—
poison ivy tagging the cypresses, the big hickory tree,
pipsissewa, buttonbush, sweetspire.
Spanish moss was always good for an hour
of fact and rumor and faint memory
after ham sandwiches and lemonade.
Did it or did it not suck the life
from the trees? Facts and counter-facts
deployed like chessmen, but it was always
a draw.

For southern ladies, for all of us
life is always a draw, but when we leave our
mark, pack our afternoons and the car trunk
with newspaper, damp around the transplanted roots,
dig a hole, watch the osprey circling the white sky,
note the world's particulars,
the scalloped flight of the pileated woodpecker,

the kingfisher's rattle, the way waterstriders dimple the surface
in this small kingdom where all things shift each hour
yet the patterns stay the same,
three o'clock's shadow in mid-May always paints
these exact triangles of light across the porch,
the benches on the pier, turtles lined up
on the same old log,
a draw is as good as a win.

Fishing at Johns Pond

"This box is being cheated. Pay
before you fish
not after. $ 1.00"

The trotline was Tojo's, pulled in
hand over hand, catfish tossed
into the bucket.

Most everyone else just dropped a baited hook
for crappie and bream. Fishing privileges
a dollar, or permission, or cleaning the spillway,
or membership in just about anything.

Sut and Old Dad went to flyfishing school,
showed off their certificates, and, mockery be damned,
sent their lines out in sizzling parabolas of light
popping bugs settled amid the mosquitoes
with a liquid tap.

Fishing is what you make it.
It takes all kinds.

Dan Wetmore

Nocturnal Phases

Old Man Moon
On time and space
Did beam with sallow,
Ravaged face...
No place to call
Another's home,
He alone
To all was known.

And all who knew
His timeless state
Would curse, and quake,
And moan their fate;
That they must pass
While he lived on
Til break of day,
From time's first dawn.

But Moon admonished
Groundlings low -
"You miss the fates
That we each know;
For one must feel
But one's demise,
While I, on the night
Of a world must rise..."

Mad Cats (Feline Opine)

A mad cat stares at me through basement window
Having found my hiding.
Angry orb eyes accusing dereliction,
For I have hefted two outside
Into the unsustaining wilds,
While I sit cozy within
At the unimportance of scratching flat white
With pointy grey
 In the magical ether of quiet
 Spun from the wakelessness of son one and son too
 Which spell the incensed ravings of felines,
  Crazed for morning's promise of full bellies,
  Would surely shatter.

When the Past Also Passes

Rainy Wednesday Night Following the Razing of the Neiswander
Farm—11 January 2006

Tonight it poured on the bones of a house
Truest fruit of a man's labor
Set fertile in the midst of a field
Of other plantings

Once wonder of shaped space,
Balanced brick and sustained span
Now slumped hillock of no interior,
Admitting nothing more.
Even entertainment of what it might have been

And yet I know on,
Having ascended diagonally so,
Having tramped across that mid-air some way
Having set my eyes from that height there ...

What are stairs but ladder-with-no-hands,
Floor but tightrope reassuringly always ahead,
And window other than frame to call sight a view?
Walls just guides to move in a space again and again,
Until muscles take on memory
To call it "ours" and us "its"
And "home" is finally knit up
From the weaving together
Of "house" and "time"
All unraveled with the pulling of threads.

Tonight drops fell
To speed the settling,
Level the evidence a little more with their pelting,
Dispatch sting of memory
In diluting deluge.

And yet, I can't but be held
By what beheld,
Having passed without pardon
Through ghosts so palpable,
Perhaps for having been likewise—
Apparition of others' future
In unavoidable trespass
Across such intangible distance
Of time-only remove.

Tonight rains wet un-remembering earth
One hundred and thirty-two seasons
Blanketed from sky.
To refresh parched land denied its embrace overlong?
To hope coax forth successor plant of shingle and door
Grown so accustomed?
I don't know.

All I do ... ?

... that mine has been a journey
Of ever turning from home;
A path which companion longing
Gifts incredulity
That others would not only leave theirs,
But spurn evidence of There having been,

... and that the element of the stuff
Which leaks from eyes,
Let down as veil across seeing,
In abundance fell
Tonight.

1700 Mail Call in Incirlik, Turkey

Your words paint a picture
that mind's eye sees a window
and the focal depth of 10 inches
becomes 7,000 miles.

But I injudiciously
drop the page
before the preoccupation,
raise my eyes
before my defenses,
and the

distance   proximity
                    to
        here   there
   appears   disappears
                   with
    alarming   astonishing
    alacrity   clarity
        and I wonder
    the wonder of all.

And here,
in the shoreless midst
of the Other
miss the immensity
of the Known,
which—
despite   due to
        remove—
    eclipses that.

Jennifer Hitch Samulski

Ode to St. Andrews

"If your daughter likes to write, she should go to St. Andrews!"

Twelve words
That changed
Everything.

The trajectory of my life
Turned that day.
And I wasn't even there.
The man,
I don't remember who he was,
A stranger to me,
Told my dad
That I should consider
This small place by the lake.

The trajectory
Redirected.

Convinced by the letters
That came to my house
Addressed to me
And not, "Dear applicant."

Convinced by the sweet lady in admissions
Who'd ask me

If I'd learned my lines for the senior play
And told me the dogwoods were blooming.

Convinced by the possibility
That one day
I could be studying poetry
In a castle, in the Italian Alps
(Me? A girl from Sugar Hollow
with only one airplane ride to my name)

Convinced by an esoteric pull
Like some cosmic invite saying,
"You belong here."

I made this place my home.

How to explain it? To an outsider? How could I?

"A place where everybody knows your name."
That's been done before.

A place where a simple walk across the lake
Is the path to everything you thought you knew
About yourself, your faith, your culture
And everything you're about to learn

A place where birthdays mean a baptism
In Lake Ansley C. Moore
(And cursing that your birthday is in January,
And not in June!)

A place where a religion major and a chemist debate

The challenges of homelessness,
And wind up in the Guinness Book of World Records

A place to unlearn the word "disabled"
And replace it with a fun word, like "wheelie"

A place with its own geography
Vardell, Detamble, Farrago, Champs, Jim's
(And at Jim's you could still play "Dirty Diana"
On the jukebox.)

The only place
Where you'd wear flip-flops
To an Extravaganza

A place to be challenged
Not so much for the right answers
But the right questions

A place for upside down Christmas trees
And a room where you can
Move the furniture

A place to sing in a choral group
And play rugby
And do lighting for a play
And mentor an at-risk child
And work at the St. Andrews Press
And learn golf, and chess, and spades
While double majoring and studying abroad.

This place screams,

"Yes, you can!"
A place for cross-cultural connections
Whether you're interested in turtles in the Galapagos
Or paintings in Florence

A place where the sound of bagpipes
Means you have arrived
And puffs you up with pride

A place where a poet, an equestrian, and a soccer player
Walk into a bar
It's not a joke
It's just a day, like any other
Where our differences were celebrated.
We were a quirky conglomeration.

A place to be fully authenticated
As an original.

"And you would never get tired of that place."

Ezra was right.

Dana Hughes

Old Man with Cracker

In a booth in a corner of a diner beside a woman
with smooth skin, an old man sat with a cracker
in one hand and a knife tipped with butter in the
other and he buttered that cracker from north to
south and east to west and all points in between,
and though he seemed to listen to the woman
while she talked and pushed things around on her
plate, it was clear he was preoccupied as he worked
the butter into every dimple, enveloping each grain
of salt in a creamy coat 'til the cracker nearly groaned
with desire for consummation, methodically moving
ever-outward 'til he reached the edge and stopped,
his thoughts drifting perhaps to a time when sailors
lived with the fear of sailing over the brink to where
ships plied the bounding main of sky and nothing more,
and what sort of shout would the mariners give to signal
the need to come about as though "man overboard" could
be expanded to include an entire vessel gone past the
boundary of the sea, but then, half-smiling, he considered
that if the cracker was the earth and the earth wasn't flat
after all, he was going to need a lot more butter.

Empty Nesting Indeed

After the children went to college and kept going
we became empty nesters, a term I dislike and a
ridiculous way to speak of oneself when the nest
is anything but empty. It's full of the chaff they
winnowed when they packed what they needed
for the school years and the after-that years.

There are beds we thought they'd want but don't,
shoes hardly worn in every size and color, boy, girl,
formal, sport, tap, cleat, high- and low-heeled, leather
and canvas veiled with dust beneath racks of suits,
shirts, dresses and sweaters that slide to the edge of
hangers like snake skin draped on a rock.

There are reliquaries of baby teeth, and first shoes,
tiny forks and tiny spoons, thread-bare blankets that
they shucked and outgrew, games missing pieces, dolls
missing clothes, a billion bits of Legos and the huddle
of basketballs slowly growing cracked and flat. These
are the things that remain when fledglings have flown.

I built this nest like the other birds, lashing twig to twig
with spider web and lining the core with down and
leaves, but the sweat of my hands, the milk of my breast
and the underpinning of prayer were my invention, and
I bound the form with lengths of my hair, dark at the
center and white toward the rim.

This nest is hardly empty, holding much of them still,
but even more it holds the all of us, the we that we made
and the us that we were when we fluffed and feathered
a tender fortress made to cup them as they hatched,
a sanctuary built for us, to secure the first thing we birthed:
our love.

The Time Had Come

I braided my hair today
after I took it from the box
in which it had lain for
more than forty years after
I insisted on cutting it for
the first time just before
my senior year of high
school because I thought
a senior year required a
sacrifice or change, however
one might choose to think.
That day the scissors opened
wide to slice through the auburn
river that ran constant
down my back every day that I
could remember, and when they
snicked shut, there sat a stranger,
a woman, holding my girlhood
in a limp puddle on her lap.
At school my classmates only
blinked and wondered why,
and I said it seemed like the
time had come, as it did again
today when I opened the box
and braided the hank like I
was standing in front of myself,
then carried it outside, nestled
it in the crook of limb and tree
and left if for the birds.

Buzzard

As it turned out,
the old man walking at a tilt
along the road, with shoulders
hunched high, bare bald head
thrust low between, and knobbed
fingers twined for balance behind
as if he might blow over in a heap
if he stood straight, though there
was no wind to bend him, despite
the sound of leafless limbs in near
trees clacking as they scraped
a bruise upon the patch of sky above,
was a buzzard,
after all, advancing toward the city
that would neither shelter like chicks
beneath a mother's wings, nor exhale
the breath sucked in when, untied,
the borrowed colt of a donkey
began to bray.

Poem Prompted by an Epigraph from Steven Taylor

Like Dido's last lament, o heavenly sound
The gentle rhythm of it doesn't Pound.

A sonnet's reply to sonnets, ending,
A thought of brave Aeneas going on
To fulfill gods' (and Virgil's) commanding;
And then—Time's differences collapsed—a boon:
A sense of Ezra, recalled from a day
When Tyrolean sun, mild in snowless
December, guided a young traveler
To a room where the old Imagist's eyes
In that white clinic-room seemed black (and glance
Serious), the man's white hair an aureole.
He said there'd been an Aquinas map once
Dante knew, and talk changed after a while.

A final tercet should be demanded,
Dante-wise... but... Metro Station... I'm reminded...

J. Hunter Patterson

When the Sun Rises

When the sun rises,
tell me your dream,
sigh with your memory
of the other world,
when the sun sets.

Let it be the same sun
that looks over the noon sky,
under a plume of atmosphere,
with a withered countenance,
the same sun that travels
the side of Earth I live on
every day, the same sun.

Let the sun be over your shoulder
as I rest on the beach,
that beautiful tattoo
hidden from view,
that picture of life
that draws me in,
under the sun rising.

Thomas Heffernan

Soon It Will Be Ten Years: Lines Written on Sept. 4, 2011

Now and then, during the last hour,
when I have glanced out the window,
the dove has been there, the same spot
on the same telephone wire,
a shade of gray, scarcely moving.
The color and the bird reminds
and doesn't remind of a day
when morning broke, from blue to gray.

The dove on the wire is alone.
Uncommon, and odd: every dove
I've seen before was with a mate.
And something else I'd seen comes back—
a wire stretched between the towers,
the aerialist walking it
back and forth, the marvel of mind
and skill and maybe luck that wind

or misstep hadn't plummeted
him headlong down through breathless air.
Another singular being;
he chose to occupy his time
doing what he alone could do.
He took a more visible way
than most, who, also, every one,
have one life, one time, that's their own.

This early September Sunday,
so near to the day of the tenth

year, I pray for those whose bodies,
in desperate courage, not to burn
alive, plummeted; pray for all
who died; and hope for those suffering
loss and memory of loss, that they
have faith love did not die that day.

I look out the window. The dove
has gone, has flown. The words *mourning
dove* come to mind, and how, native
where accent sounded them alike,
as a boy I had wondered if
the bird's name wasn't *morning dove.*
Now, both feelings are connecting:
I mourn; I'm glad it is morning.

A Narrative Poem Which Concerns the Clifton Suspension Bridge, Two Hundred Feet High, Near Bristol in England, During the Latter Part of the Nineteenth Century

Her husband rebukes her breach of etiquette.
She does nothing, staying meek, silent.
And then walks to the bridge. Hoists her skirts.
Stands on the rail midway. And jumps.

At once, beginning to pray sideways,
She feels a loss of control. This haze.
That brute. Arms and legs collide,
Come right, beseech disappearing God.

Goodness, goodness, the children's voices.
One angry, one sad, her husband's faces.
Her stays are pinching hard.
Smelling-salts she wants, and food.

Skirts ballooning, she almost stops.
Clutches bosoms; smooths, weeps.
Bitter, these last regrets. Oh, God,
She calls, being very bold, God!

Gracious, how cautious and slow,
The air, as it slides from below,
Over high stockings, lifts up skirts,
Makes bloomers bloom so much it hurts.

A shock, and then her feet, in its grasp,
Feel the gelatin-mud sumping her to a creep.
It shakes and shimmers at the tops
Of her legs, and then, at her buttocks, stops.

Later, the couple are reconciled.
They promenade the bridge, much besmiled.
Arm in arm they walk. Pleasant. Silent.
She is smiling, a portrait of Victorian etiquette.

They walk arm in arm. Gracious. Pleasant.
Portraits of Victorian etiquette, both are silent.
After they have passed, people say, Isn't it super,
Knowing the first Victorian lady paratrooper?

Her husband, dutiful, smiles back.
His expression shows tact, a lack
Of any talent for the extreme.
She twirls her parasol; looks serene.

Pilot

Do you believe a flight will be off course
almost a hundred percent of the time?
The automatic pilot like a mime
(of me) brings it back on course, like the boss
it truly is, except for landing and take-off.
Off course so much, but guided, I'm assured
is true, true as fact? as metaphor? Blurred,
I ask myself does it matter what rough
bent of meaning applies, so long as right
aeronautics do? My brother says math
is full of paradox, like the weird truth
that one system has parallel lines to meet
at infinity, what I could say is true
when deep cloud breaks into endless blue.

Contributors

Dobree Adams, recognized as one of Kentucky's major contemporary fiber artists, weaves one-of-a-kind rugs and tapestries from her handspun yarns. She spins and dyes the wool from a rare breed of sheep, the Lincoln Longwood, an old British breed renowned for the curl, luster, strength, and length of its wool.

Through the years she has taken hundreds of photographs, primarily as 35mm color slides, to record the images she has gathered, at home on the farm as well as in her travels. These slides have rarely been used in the design process, but rather to demonstrate the influences behind her woven work. In her slide lectures she has brought together images of her weavings and images of landscape. She is now committed to working in photography as well as in fiber. "I am fascinated by the landscape and how light changes the contours and colors from dawn to dusk and from season to season. I never tire of watching and recording how the light falls on the hills behind our river bottom, of how light creates layers of trees and mist and fog."

Lyrics by **Dick Bakken**, 55, leader of Intergenerational Poetry & Performance Workshop conceived by lyricist—scored, arranged, sung by Judy Melody, 17, Douglas, Arizona; with chorus Rosemary Snapps, 68, Hereford, Arizona; Cody Dickson, 13, Bisbee, Arizona; A.J.

Morales, 11, Bisbee, Arizona—with keyboard, Ben Caron, 21, Hereford, Arizona—performed at Summer Writers Camp Showcase, Bisbee Repertory Theatre, on August 16, 1997, Bisbee, Arizona.

Joseph Bathanti is a poet, a writer, a scholar, and a professor at Appalachian State University who has written numerous essays about Black Mountain College. He has published seven collections of poetry, most recently *Concertina* (2013). He has published one collection of short stories and three novels, most recently *The Life of the World to Come* (2014). Bathanti, originally from Pittsburgh, Pennsylvania, first came to North Carolina in 1976 to hold writing workshops in prisons as part of the VISTA (Volunteers in Service to America) program. He remained here and became our North Carolina Poet Laureate from 2012-2014. During his tenure, he championed working with veterans in North Carolina suffering from Post-Traumatic-Stress Syndrome through writing programs designed to be therapeutic. In September Joseph will be honored by receiving the Governor's Medal, the state's most prestigious award, for his achievement in literature. However, most importantly, Joseph Bathanti is a long-standing friend of St. Andrews.

Brenda Butka practices poetry and pulmonary medicine in Nashville, Tennessee. She has published in *The Threepenny Review, Slant, Cortland Review, Florida Review, Chest, JAMA, TicToc,* and elsewhere.

She married into the John family and therefore nearly considers herself from Laurinburg.

Jonathan Greene, born in New York City, earned his BA in literature from Bard College in Annandale-on-Hudson, New York, where he studied American literature with Ralph Ellison. He went on to study poetry with Robert Lowell and folklore with Alan Dundes. The author of more than 30 chapbooks and volumes of poetry, Greene has run Gnomon Press since 1965. He currently works as a freelance designer in Kentucky. He has received many design awards, including honors from the American Association of University Presses, the Chicago Book Clinic, the Midwest Book Show, and the Southern Books Competition.

Whit Griffin holds a BA from Bennington College and an MFA from Brooklyn College. His most valuable "schooling," however, came from his mentorship with the poet Theodore Enslin and his time as a Jargon Society intern for Jonathan Williams and Thomas Meyer, both poets as well as editors.

He has published four books: *Penateuch: The First Five Books*; *The Sixth Great Extinction*; *A Far-Shining Crystal*; and *We Who Saw Everything*. Recent work has appeared in *Chicago Review*, *Hambone*, *Golden Handcuffs Review* and *The Doris*.

He has the unique position of having studied with Ron Bayes, Theodore Enslin, Jonathan Williams, and Thomas Meyer. His work is rooted in mysticism, mythology, ethno-botany and the esoteric. His poetry deals with flux and metamorphosis, uncertainty and ambiguity, sentience and spirituality, especially the intersection of the spiritual realm and the physical realm. The poems aim to de-compartmentalize the psychic life and to reach a state when knowledge itself becomes a mystery. He writes in a non-linear style, relying on collage and juxtaposition. His poems do not attempt to answer any questions. But in the participatory act of reading, the consciousness of the reader is altered and changed. And in that altered state new possibilities may be imagined.

Thomas Heffernan's *Liam Poems* received the Roanoke-Chowan Prize (1982). Other awards—for poems, essay, play writing—include the 2006 Kusamakura Grand Prize for haiku. He has published widely in the United States and Japan. *Working Voices*, his collection of seventy-five monologues, appeared in 2016.

Dana Hughes is a wife, mother of three grown children, keeper of many pets, a poet, quilter, knitter, and keen observer of myriad aspects of life. She lives in Atlanta, Georgia.

Basil King is a poet and artist who has had over 50 art exhibitions and has published 16 books of poetry. His artwork is in the following institutions: Yale University, Wadsworth Athenaeum, State University of New York at Buffalo, Spencer Collection at The New York Public Library, North Carolina State Museum of Art, Black Mountain College Museum & Art Center, and the Asheville Art Museum, to mention a few. Some of his most recent books are *Grey* and *The Spoken Word/The Painted Hand*, both from *Learning to Draw/A History*, and *Portraits*. Basil King also describes himself thus: "I think I began to draw when I was 5 or 6 years old. I remember copying cartoons by David Low. Black and white. Black and white has always been very important to me. Ink. Charcoal. Print. By the time I was 14 I was painting every day. But otherwise, as has often been the case, my life was unsettled and difficult. By lucky circumstance, I found Black Mountain College when I was 16—and from there I was able to enter New York City and San Francisco. I often explain my art by saying 'from the abstract to the figure, from the figure to the abstract makes an edge of exquisite distance and distance gives us our sensations.' Writing was part of being at Black Mountain. But I did not begin to write seriously until 1985, after a series of disappointments followed by my first trip back to England since my parents and I emigrated in 1947. When I returned to New York, I could not stop writing. It was 'a season of digestion.' Today I go back and forth between painting and writing, on two different floors of my house in Brooklyn. One feeds the other and in both I bring disparate things together."

Martha King is a poet and prose writer who has had over 50 pieces published in various periodicals and journals, most recently in *Skidrow Penthouse*, *Blaze Vox*, and the essay "Single with Others" that will be forthcoming in the anthology *The Wreckage of Reason: Back to the Drawing Board*. She describes herself thus: "I am a writer because of my small place in American history, as a middleclass white female 'bohemian' who has lived an unspeakably orderly life, held down full time jobs, paid taxes and a mortgage, lived in the same house in Brooklyn, New York, for more than 30 years, and raised kids to hold up all kinds of old WASP virtues: honesty, table manners, love of justice, good grammar. I am a writer because my small place in American history began in Jamestown and most of it centered in the Southern United States, hip deep in the stain of chattel slavery and all its ugly descendants and lulled by the story-telling traditions and linguistic seductions common to that territory."

The poetry of **Peter McNamara** has appeared in numerous journals and is gathered in four collections and, most recently, *Orbit's Crossing* and *Sixteen Poems*, chapbooks published by St. Andrews University Press. He lectures currently in the OLLI adult learning program at Eckerd College in St. Petersburg.

Thomas Meyer is a poet, translator, and editor. He was born in 1947 and grew up in Seattle, Washington. He received his B.A. in English from Bard College in Annandale-on-the-Hudson, New York. He has ten books of poetry published, most recently *Modern Love: Songs* (2014) and *Kintsugi* (2011). He translated *Lizard: Or Easy Answers They are None Being a Novel Tracing of the I Ching* (2013) and *Beowulf: A Translation* (2012). He had been the co-editor of the Jargon Press with Jonathan Williams for over forty years. He lives in Highlands, North Carolina.

Peter O'Leary describes his poetry: "Meyer is a poet of impeccable musical skills and visionary incisiveness; through his work, you can trace a clear line from Jonathan Williams through Bunting to Pound and back of Pound to the Pre-Raphaelites, to the Provencal poets and Dante, and to the Romans, the Greeks, and the Chinese in antiquity."

J. Hunter Patterson (1952-1996) was a Georgia-born writer who graduated from St. Andrews College in 1977 with a degree in modern languages. Fluent in Spanish, he also studied at the University of the Americas (Cholula, Mexico) and at the University of Georgia School of Law, where he earned a law degree in the early 1980s. He lived in San Jose, Costa Rica; Athens, Georgia; and Atlanta, Georgia, where he maintained a career specializing in real-estate title law during his thirties. He was a prolific writer throughout his twenties and thirties, although he never seemed concerned with publishing his work. He is the author of "It is Okay to Sleep Now," a poem published as a St. Andrews chapbook in 1977, during which year he also edited the St. Andrews student literary magazine, *Cairn*. Some of his poems appeared in issues of that magazine as well as in *St. Andrews Review* and the *Red Hand Book* anthologies published by Atlanta-based Pynyon Press (1979-1982). His visionary memoir *The Banks of Hunger and Hardship (A Map of Time)* was posthumously published in 2003 by Spuyten Duyvil (New York).

Tom Patterson is a St. Andrews alum who was a senior in 1974 for the first Black Mountain College Festival. As curator, he has organized group and solo exhibitions for institutions including the American Visionary Art Museum, the Southeastern Center for Contemporary Art, Virginia Commonwealth University's Anderson Gallery, and the Jamaica Center for Arts and Learning to name a few. He is also the author of several color-illustrated books: *Howard Finster: Stranger from Another World*, *St. EOM in The Land of Pasaquan*, and *Contemporary Folk Art: Treasures from the Smithsonian American Art Museum*. His latest book is the catalog for the exhibition "Farfetched: Mad Science, Fringe Architecture and Visionary Engineering," which he co-curated with Roger Manley in 2013 at N.C. State University's Gregg Museum of Art & Design in Raleigh, North Carolina.

Following a stint in the Army Air Corps, where **Simon Perchik** served as a pilot, he enrolled in New York University under the GI Bill and began writing poetry. After receiving a B.A. in English, he went straight to NYU Law School. From 1950 until 1980 Perchik practiced law, while continuing to write poetry. He was

Suffolk County Long Island's first Environmental Prosecutor.

I Counted Only April was published in 1964. Fifteen collections followed. In 2000, he released a compilation of all his earlier books with *Hands Collected: The Books of Simon Perchik (Poems 1949-1999)*. It was nominated for the National Book Award. That same year he brought out *Touching the Headstone* and most recently *The Autochthon Poems*.

Perchik has placed hundreds of poems in journals and periodicals that include *The New Yorker*, *Poetry*, *Partisan Review*, and *The Nation*. He resides in East Hampton, New York, with the rest of his family.

Jennifer Hitch Samulski was born in Asheville, NC, and has lived in many small towns throughout the state. During her time at St. Andrews, Jennifer had many opportunities to be creative, including a semester abroad at Brunnenburg, Italy. Jennifer has a M.A. in Clinical Psychology from Appalachian State University and a certificate in School Counseling from NC A&T State University. Jennifer has worked for 24 years in the field of children's mental health, and is currently a school counselor at Randleman Elementary School. She has two children, Hayley and Sean, and resides in Greensboro.

Dan Wetmore spent his formative years in the halcyon hold of Laurinburg, N.C., where he earned a B.A. from

Saint Andrews Presbyterian College in 1986, followed by an M.A. from Bowling Green State University, then parlayed dual degrees in Philosophy into a twenty-year career in the Air Force, including tours of duty on nuclear alert in a missile silo, launching satellites aboard decommissioned ICBMs, as an instructor of Logic and Ethics at the Air Force Academy, and overseeing a Communications Post in southern Turkey.

Having landed in Albuquerque N.M., he's now self-"employed," dividing days between the exploits of a wonderful wife and two enterprising sons, anchoring a chair at a local Starbucks under the pretense of writing, wrenching on various old cars, and hiking in the high desert mountains (but dreams of boomeranging back east to the land of green, seasons, and days past which seek to paint future ones).

Jonathan Williams (1929-2008), a poet, critic, editor, and photographer, dropped out of Princeton University to study at BMC in the early 1950s. He founded Jargon Press in 1951 to publish the work of poets "outside" the usual high-profile poetic circles.

As such, as Dennis Hevesi notes, "Williams was an early champion of outsider art—works by those, mostly self-taught, who are outside the artistic establishment and away from art-world centers and might use materials like corrugated roofing, plywood or rug remnants."

Williams celebrated the lesser known and the avant-garde, which means art work that is experimental or innovative—a piece of art that pushes the boundaries of what is considered acceptable or conventional.

John "Jomo" Williamson lives in New York City.

Acknowledgments

Heffernan, Thomas. "Soon it will be Ten Years: Lines Written on Sept. 4, 2011." Published on the North Carolina Arts Council website ten years after 9/11.

---. "A Narrative Poem Which Concerns the Clifton Suspension Bridge, Two Hundred Feet High, Near Bristol in England, During the Latter Part of the Nineteenth Century." First published in the collection of poetry *Mobiles*.

---. "Pilot." First published in the collection of poetry *Working Voices*.

www.ingramcontent.com/pod-product-compliance
Lightning Source LLC
Chambersburg PA
CBHW061250170626
46809CB00007B/2930